# THE GYPSY ROSE BLANCHARD STORY

A Twisted Tale of Love, Lies, Liberation and the Complex Layers of Deception and Survival

By

Cassandra T. Peters

**TABLE OF CONTENT**

Gypsy Rose Blanchard is a woman who became widely known for her participation in a convoluted and sorrowful incident of deceit and mistreatment. Gypsy Rose, born in 1991, resided in Springfield, Missouri with her mother, Dee Dee Blanchard who appeared to be the epitome of a devoted caretaker.

Dee Dee portrayed Gypsy Rose as being seriously unwell, both in terms of physical and mental health, asserting that Gypsy Rose was afflicted with various conditions such as leukemia, muscular dystrophy, and cognitive impairments.

Over the course of numerous years, the community united in support of the Blanchards, offering monetary aid, presents, and even a place to live. Gypsy Rose frequently appeared in a wheelchair, appearing to rely on her mother for assistance. Nevertheless, the actual essence of the affair was a somber and unsettling narrative of mistreatment.

The revelation regarding Gypsy and her mother's situation surfaced subsequent to Gypsy orchestrating the homicide of Dee Dee through an online boyfriend in 2015.

The Gypsy Rose Blanchard Story is a captivating narrative that provokes contemplation on the intricacies of abuse and the extreme measures someone may go to liberate themselves from such circumstances.

# CHAPTER ONE

## Dee Dee Blanchard at Young Age

At first glance, Dee Dee Blanchard appeared to be the epitome of a devoted caretaker. She was an unmarried mother who went to great lengths to assist her profoundly unwell daughter, Gypsy Rose Blanchard.

When Dee Dee was discovered brutally murdered at her Missouri residence in June 2015, it caused much shock and horror, particularly because Gypsy Rose, who is confined to a wheelchair, was nowhere to be found. However, the police quickly discovered that Dee Dee was not the affectionate mother she portrayed herself to be. On the contrary, for over twenty years, she had brutally treated her daughter Gypsy Rose in the medical system, making up a litany of ailments that she did not actually have and then "taking care" of her.

As opposed to previous beliefs, Gypsy Rose Blanchard was not actually ill and had the ability to walk without any difficulty, despite her reliance on a wheelchair. Instead of benefiting her, her mother's misguided "treatments" often caused harm. Furthermore, it was Gypsy Rose herself who orchestrated the murder of her mother. Upon learning of

Dee Dee Blanchard's horrific death, acquaintances of hers shared numerous accounts that unveil a profoundly unsettling portrayal of the life and end of a mother afflicted with a severe instance of Munchausen syndrome by proxy.

This is her terrifying story...


Clauddine "Dee Dee" Blanchard (formerly known as Pitre) was born on May 3, 1967, in Chackbay, Louisiana. Her parents were Claude Anthony Pitre Sr. and Emma Lois Gisclair. From a young age, Dee Dee garnered notice due to her peculiar and malevolent conduct. Her own relatives expressed unfavorable opinions about her. It was said that Dee Dee frequently pilfered belongings from her relatives. In addition, they levied allegations of credit card fraud and issuing insufficient funds checks against her. Laura made a startling accusation, asserting that Dee Dee had made an attempt on her life by adding the herbicide Roundup to her diet. Laura ultimately endured the poisoning but underwent a nine-month period of recuperation. The family's assertions do not end there. Additionally, they allege that Dee Dee was responsible for the murder of her own mother, Emma. Kristy Blanchard, Gypsy Rose's stepmother, concurs with that accusation. She asserted that on the day her mother passed away, Dee Dee was there at the residence and deliberately depriving her of food.

Despite the scarcity of physical evidence, the authenticity of these accusations is widely believed due to the appalling mistreatment that Dee Dee Blanchard inflicted upon her daughter in later years. Dee Dee ultimately relocated from her family, pursuing a career as a nurse's aide and entering into a romantic relationship with Rod Blanchard, who was seven years younger than her.

# CHAPTER TWO

## Early Life of Rose Blanchard

Nomad Rose Blanchard was raised by her mother, Dee Dee Blanchard, who consistently made assertions about her health, leading to a sequence of severe diagnoses and medical treatments. Contrary to what was claimed, Gypsy was not truly ill; her mother had been deceitful about her symptoms. Dee Dee's actions were believed to be a result of the mental ailment known as Munchausen syndrome by proxy. This sickness involves a person pretending and causing illness in another individual, in this case, Dee Dee's daughter, as Dee Dee desired to play the role of a caregiver.

Furthermore, it constitutes a type of child maltreatment. It impacts caregivers, particularly those who care for youngsters. It is alternatively referred to as factitious disorder by proxy. This disorder primarily affects mothers with young children. Paternal figures or other individuals responsible for caregiving might also experience it. An individual afflicted with Munchausen syndrome by proxy (MSP) will exhibit behavior that mimics the illness of the person they are responsible for.

They frequently manipulate medical data. They might deceive medical professionals on the health or state of the individual under their supervision. They engage in this behavior to elicit pity or to seek attention.

## Munchausen Syndrome by Proxy (MSP)

An individual with Munchausen syndrome by proxy (MSP) may intentionally engage in behaviors to induce illness in their child. They deliberately subject the youngster to painful or risky medical procedures, including operations. They may intentionally induce symptoms in a child. They can achieve this by depriving the child of food, administering poison or smothering the child, administering incorrect medications, or withholding recommended medications. Engaging in such circumstances can expose the child to significant peril. Individuals with MSP are not deterred by the financial burden of medical treatments. They are unconcerned about the management of their bills. On the contrary, they hold the belief that incurring a substantial medical expense serves to strengthen the idea that parents are exerting maximum effort to ensure the well-being of their child. They believe that others will perceive them as superior caregivers.

Identifying symptoms of MSP might be challenging. There exist specific personality traits and backgrounds that appear to be prevalent. A significant number of individuals experienced psychological, physiological, or sexual mistreatment during their formative years. Alternatively, they were only shown affection or given attention when they were unwell.

Adults with MSP exhibit a profound fascination with the field of medicine. They frequently work in the healthcare industry. They possess advanced knowledge and proficiency in discussing medical conditions. They generally exhibit a high level of cooperation and friendliness towards health care workers. They consistently demonstrate unwavering dedication to the welfare of their child.

However, in order to feign symptoms of disease in their child, parents may resort to drastic measures. Some examples of these could be:

- Administering emetic or laxative chemicals to induce vomiting or diarrhea in the youngster.

- Manipulating thermometers to simulate an elevated body temperature in a child

- Undernourishing the infant to induce a failure to thrive.

- Presence of hematuria or melena in the child's urine or stool

In the case of a child, symptoms indicating a caregiver with Munchausen syndrome by proxy (MSP) involve a past record of frequent hospital visits due to atypical health issues. Oftentimes, their symptoms do not correspond to any specific ailment.

Symptoms typically exacerbate when individuals are in isolation with their caregiver. Symptoms frequently resolve when the individual is not present. The ethical dilemmas associated with MSP provide challenges for diagnosis.

Alleging that a mother, father, or caretaker deliberately induces symptoms or causes illness in a kid is a grave issue. An effective method to validate suspicions of Munchausen syndrome by proxy (MSP) involves isolating the child from the mother, father, or caregiver and thereafter assessing if the child's symptoms ameliorate.

Medical professionals are also capable of assessing medical documents. They can search for patterns indicative of anomalies. For instance, if a child has been diagnosed with numerous ailments within a brief timeframe, it should raise suspicion.

The treatment of the mother, father, or caregiver involved is not as simple or uncomplicated. Oftentimes, this individual will adamantly refuse to acknowledge their involvement, even in the face of compelling proof. They frequently obfuscate the distinction between truth and falsehood. Unless they are willing to acknowledge the truth, their progress will be hindered. Psychotherapy is advised for individuals who have MSP. Throughout these counseling sessions, the therapist assists the caregiver in recognizing the emotions that prompted their detrimental actions. With the passage of time, the caregiver can acquire the ability to modify that habit. They can acquire the ability to cultivate good relationships that are not contingent upon someone's illness.

# CHAPTER THREE

## A Horrific and Abusive Childhood

Gypsy's parents, Rod and Dee Dee, initially encountered each other during Rod's high school years and subsequently wedded after Dee Dee discovered her pregnancy. At that time, he was 17 years old, whilst Dee Dee was 24. They ultimately parted up shortly prior to Gypsy's birth on July 27, 1991. Gypsy Rose was an infant when Dee Dee asserted that her daughter was suffering from sleep apnea. Despite doing multiple medical examinations, physicians did not identify any abnormalities in Gypsy. Nevertheless, Dee Dee developed a strong belief that Gypsy was suffering from an illness, ultimately informing Rod that she held the conviction that their daughter possessed a chromosomal abnormality, which was the root cause of her health problems. Over time, her beliefs regarding Gypsy's ailments escalated, reaching a stage where she erroneously asserted that Gypsy had leukemia and muscular dystrophy.

At the age of 8, Gypsy was characterized by Dee Dee as afflicted with leukemia and muscular dystrophy, necessitating the use of a wheelchair and a feeding tube. Dee Dee provided a comprehensive account of her daughter's medical issues, which encompassed seizures, asthma, as well as hearing and vision impairments. As a result of Dee Dee's activities, Gypsy was prescribed a multitude of drugs and required the use of a breathing apparatus during sleep. In addition, she underwent several surgical interventions, including ophthalmic procedures and excision of her salivary glands. Gypsy's teeth were extracted when they decayed, possibly as a result of her drugs, absence of salivary glands, or lack of care. However, it was a fact that Gypsy has the ability to walk, did not require a feeding tube, and was not afflicted with cancer. The reason for her bald head was solely due to her mother's act of shaving off her hair. Dee Dee is thought to have suffered from Munchausen syndrome by proxy, this behavior was motivated by her desire to garner attention and sympathy for her role as a caregiver to a sick child.

Medical testing frequently yielded equivocal or conflicting outcomes in relation to Gypsy's diagnosis. However, Dee Dee would discontinue consultations with any doctors who expressed doubts about her daughter's illnesses. Numerous caregivers acquiesced to Dee Dee's desires. With her background in nursing, she had the ability to provide precise descriptions of symptoms and occasionally administered medication to Gypsy in order to simulate specific medical conditions.

Dee Dee exhibited charm and appeared to be deeply committed to her daughter. Once Gypsy reached an age where she could communicate, Dee Dee explicitly encouraged her to refrain from providing any further information at their medical checkups. It was always Dee Dee who fabricated Gypsy's medical history. Gypsy's father Rod Blanchard, praised Dee Dee for her unwavering dedication. Upon observing that Gypsy did not appear to require a wheelchair, several members of Dee Dee's family inquired about the matter. Consequently, Dee Dee and Gypsy relocated.

Dee Dee and Gypsy's residence was severely damaged as a consequence of Hurricane Katrina. Subsequently, they visited a rescue center where Dee Dee asserted that all of Gypsy's medical records, including her birth certificate, were obliterated during the hurricane. This created an opportunity for Dee Dee to further deceive others regarding Gypsy's health and age. Dee Dee asserted herself as a Hurricane Katrina survivor, which led to her and Gypsy receiving aid to move from Louisiana to Missouri in 2005. Dee Dee persistently accompanied Gypsy to medical visits.

# CHAPTER FOUR

## An Act of Deception

Following Hurricane Katrina, Dee Dee and Gypsy eventually moved to Springfield, Missouri, after being provided with a tiny home by Habitat for Humanity. Gypsy's story garnered media coverage, resulting in a substantial influx of support for the mother-daughter pair, including numerous philanthropic donations such as complimentary vacations to Walt Disney World and exclusive access to Miranda Lambert performances. The house, constructed by Habitat for

Humanity, was adorned with a pink hue and featured a ramp to facilitate handicapped access. Gypsy and Dee Dee also obtained privileges which encompassed philanthropy-funded excursions to concerts and Disney World. Throughout the entire time, Dee Dee consistently enjoyed the admiration she earned for being a dedicated caregiver.

At the age of 14, Gypsy consulted a neurologist in Missouri who eventually concluded that she was suffering from Munchausen syndrome via proxy. Nevertheless, this doctor failed to notify the authorities about her condition.

During subsequent interviews, he expressed his conviction that there was insufficient proof to take action. In 2009, an undisclosed report was submitted to authorities, asserting that Dee Dee's descriptions of Gypsy's illnesses had no medical foundation.

As a consequence, two caseworkers conducted a house visit, although Dee Dee successfully persuaded them that there were no issues. As Gypsy aged, Dee Dee started fabricating her own age, even resorting to modifying the dates on Gypsy's birth certificate to portray her daughter as younger. However, Gypsy was increasingly challenging for Dee Dee to manage.

Gypsy's existence was characterized by her mother's constant supervision and manipulation. She was prohibited from attending school. Despite Gypsy had average cognitive abilities, Dee Dee falsely claimed that her daughter had a mental age equivalent to that of a 7-year-old. During public outings, Dee Dee consistently grasped Gypsy's hand, exerting pressure on it to signal her desire for her daughter to be silent.

## Dee Dee. Blanchard's Murder

In 2011, Gypsy attempted to escape from her mother by eloping with an individual she had encountered at a science fiction conference. However, Dee Dee promptly located them through shared acquaintances. She persuaded the man that Gypsy was underage, despite her true age of 19 at the time. Gypsy alleges that upon their return home, Dee Dee forcefully damaged her computer and violently confined her to her bed. Gypsy has moreover asserted that her mother would occasionally physically assault her and withhold nourishment.

Gypsy ultimately succeeded in reconnecting to the internet. She enrolled in a Christian dating platform, where she encountered Nicholas Godejohn. She disclosed the truth regarding her mother's deeds to him and ultimately requested him to eliminate Dee Dee in order for them to unite.

On June 9, 2015, Godejohn flew to Missouri to rendezvous with Gypsy. He patiently waited for Gypsy to indicate that Dee Dee was asleep before he entered their residence. Once Dee Dee had fallen asleep, Godejohn proceeded to enter the premises. Gypsy, in turn, sought refuge in a bathroom while

Godejohn carried out the act of fatally stabbing Dee Dee.

Gypsy and Godejohn were apprehended by the authorities at his residence in Wisconsin. Gypsy had made two posts on the Facebook account she shared with her mother. In one of the posts, she wrote, "That woman is deceased!" Subsequently, she clarified that she had created the posts with the intention of facilitating the discovery of her mother's body. Following Dee Dee's homicide, some individuals acquainted with Gypsy questioned the extent to which she had gone in order to do the act. From the moment she gained the ability to walk, she possessed the capability to publicly reveal Dee Dee's falsehoods by simply standing up. However, Gypsy had been indoctrinated to believe that nobody would trust her account. She elucidated, "I refrained from abruptly exiting the wheelchair due to apprehension and uncertainty regarding my mother's potential reaction." I lacked a reliable confidant.

Dee Dee's pals became immediately concerned upon seeing the post she wrote about her deceased mother. Upon their unsuccessful attempts to establish communication with Dee Dee, they promptly notified the authorities.

Subsequently, law enforcement discovered Dee Dee's deceased body within her residence. Upon discovering Dee Dee's deceased body, law enforcement successfully traced the IP address of the Facebook posts to Big Bend, Wisconsin, the location where Gypsy and Godejohn were residing. Godejohn's family home was subjected to a police raid, resulting in the arrest of both Godejohn and Gypsy on charges of murder and felony armed criminal action. Subsequent to the demise of Dee Dee and the apprehension of Gypsy, additional information emerged regarding Gypsy's status as a victim of

Munchausen via proxy. Eventually, it became evident to the world that Gypsy Rose Blanchard was not the ill girl her mother portrayed her to be, but rather a robust and thriving young woman. During the murder, Gypsy Rose, who was 23 years old, was in a generally good state of health, except for minor problems that were likely induced by her mother, such as decayed teeth resulting from either inadequate dental care or excessive use of drugs.

The disclosure astounded acquaintances, relatives, and all those who were familiar with Gypsy Rose's story. Dee Dee Blanchard is now believed to have been afflicted with Munchausen syndrome by proxy, in order to garner attention.

# CHAPTER FIVE

## Final Release of Gypsy Rose

The trial of Godejohn took place in November 2018. Gypsy attested that she devised the scheme to eliminate her mother as it was the sole means by which she could liberate herself from a life of mistreatment. Although there was no disagreement regarding Godejohn's responsibility for Dee Dee's death, his legal representatives said that he was coerced by Gypsy into committing the act and therefore should face a lesser charge of second-degree murder.

After many days, Godejohn was convicted of premeditated murder in the June 2015 killing of Gypsy's mother. In addition, he was convicted of armed criminal action. Godejohn is presently serving a life term at Missouri's Potosi Correctional Center.

In April 2019, Gypsy became betrothed to a different individual who corresponded with her while she was incarcerated. Nevertheless, the two individuals did not enter into matrimony.

Due to the evidence of abuse recorded in Gypsy's medical records, her lawyer successfully negotiated a plea agreement for the charges she was facing in relation to Dee Dee's death. In 2016, Gypsy admitted guilt to second-degree murder. She received a 10-year prison sentence and completed 85 percent of her term before being released on December 28, 2023. Gypsy has asserted that she became aware of the full scope of her mother's deceit only after Dee Dee's demise. Although Gypsy was aware of her ability to walk and consume conventional meals, she had the belief that she was afflicted with leukemia.

Gypsy married her current spouse, Ryan Scott Anderson, while she was still incarcerated, following his correspondence with her. Anderson retrieved her following her release.

Currently, Gypsy is in good health. Additionally, she has expressed that she experienced a greater degree of autonomy while incarcerated compared to her previous existence alongside Dee Dee. Having been released from prison, Gypsy expresses her dissatisfaction with Dee Dee's demise. Gypsy communicated for the first time since her release from prison on New Year's Eve, conveying a message to her admirers. "Greetings, individuals. I am Gypsy." "I have achieved liberation," Gypsy proclaimed in a video shared on her social media. "I would want to express my gratitude through this brief film to acknowledge the overwhelming support I have received on social media. The kindness and encouragement from everyone have been truly remarkable, and I am sincerely grateful for it." "It is pleasant to be back at home." I have returned to my residence in Louisiana, relishing a splendid day outdoors, and eagerly anticipating a multitude of favorable events in the near future.

In addition, she disclosed her enthusiasm for celebrating New Year's Eve in the company of her family and spouse. "We aim to celebrate the start of the new year as a group." "It will be quite delightful to get some quality time with family after such a lengthy period," she expressed.

**END**